COUNTRY

Formal Name: Russian Federation (Rossiyskaya Federatsiya).

Short Form: Russia.

Term for Citizen(s): Russian(s).

Capital: Moscow (Moskva).

Major Cities (in order of population): St. Petersburg, Novosibirsk, Yekaterinburg, Nizhniy Novgorod, Omsk, Samara, Kazan', Chelyabinsk, Rostov-na-Donu, Ufa, Volgograd, and Perm.

Independence: Russia officially marks its independence on June 12, 1991, the date of the Russian Republic's declaration of sovereignty from the Soviet Union.

Public Holidays: Official holidays are New Year's (January 1–2), Orthodox Christmas (January 7), Women's Day (March 8), Orthodox Easter Monday (variable date in April or early May), May Day (May 1–2), Victory Day (May 9), Russia Day (Independence Day, June 12), National Unity Day (November 4), and Constitution Day (December 12).

Flag: Three equal-sized horizontal bands of white (top), red, and blue.

Click to Enlarge Image

HISTORICAL BACKGROUND

Early History: Kievan Rus', which was founded in the late ninth century, was the first state established on the territory of modern Russia. In 988 Orthodox Christianity was declared the official religion of this state, which thereafter maintained close relations with the Byzantine Empire. In the thirteenth century, a weakened and fragmented Kiev was overrun by a Mongol invasion. The Mongol occupation, which lasted until 1480, provided the conditions for a new state, Muscovy, to emerge and eclipse Kiev. Under a series of strong rulers, by 1600 Muscovy had consolidated a large portion of what later was European Russia. The concurrent decline of the Byzantine Empire led to a longstanding claim that Moscow was the "Third Rome," and an independent Russian Orthodox Church emerged in 1589.

The Romanovs: In 1613 Muscovy ended a period of political and economic hardship by naming as tsar Mikhail Romanov (r. 1613–45), whose family would rule Muscovy and then Russia for the next 300 years. After a series of weak rulers, Peter I (the Great, r. 1682–1725) emerged at the end of the seventeenth century as a powerful force for change. In a series of wars, political reforms, and extensive contacts with the West, Peter laid the foundation of the Russian Empire as a world power open to foreign cultural influences. The eighteenth century ended with another powerful monarch, Catherine II (the Great, r. 1762–96), who further expanded the empire and attempted political and social reform. By the first half of the nineteenth century, Russia was one of the most influential countries in Europe. However, Russia did not share the advances of the Industrial Revolution, and the survival of serfdom as the basis of Russian agriculture further hindered social and economic progress in this period.

Revolution and Formation of the Soviet Union: Throughout the nineteenth century, Russia was governed by autocratic rulers who suppressed revolutionary ideals imported from the West. Major social and economic reform programs in the 1860s and at the turn of the century failed to address Russia's most acute problems. In 1914, when Russia became a major participant in World War I, the economic gap between Russia and Western Europe had grown and so had dissatisfaction with the monarchy. Combined with those conditions, the stress of the war effort allowed the radical Bolshevik Party, led by Vladimir I. Lenin, to overthrow the provisional government that had displaced the tsar in 1917. At the conclusion of a bloody, four-year civil war, Russia began a 70-year period of one-party rule as the major constituent part of a new entity, the Soviet Union. At the outset, that union included Ukraine, Byelorussia, and three Transcaucasian republics; the ruling party was known as the Communist Party of the Soviet Union (CPSU).

After an initial period of confusion and experimentation, in 1927 the Soviet Union came under the control of Joseph V. Stalin. Stalin's regime became steadily more repressive in the 1930s and locked the national economy into a rigid system of state control, with five-year plans prescribing the performance of every economic sector and heavily emphasizing heavy industry. By 1939 the Soviet Union had been transformed from a primarily agricultural country into a world industrial power. From 1941 until 1944, the Soviet Union fought German invading forces in World War II, losing millions of Russian lives. After the war, the Soviet Union and the United States emerged as the world's major economic and ideological rivals in what soon came to be called the Cold War. In the early years of that confrontation, the Soviet Union gained control of all of Eastern Europe and developed a nuclear bomb. The death of Stalin in 1953 led to some domestic liberalization under Nikita Khrushchev (party leader, 1953–64), but the ideologically based confrontation with the West continued until the collapse of the Soviet Union in 1991.

Under Leonid I. Brezhnev, party leader from 1964 until 1982, major agreements brought some relief of Cold War tensions, but an 11-year Soviet occupation of Afghanistan (1979–89) minimized their effect. The accession of Mikhail S. Gorbachev as CPSU first secretary in 1985 brought major changes in domestic and international policy. Gorbachev liberalized economic, political, and media policies and fostered closer relations with the West. By 1991, however, the inherent weaknesses of the Soviet Union brought about the collapse of its East European empire and then the union itself. When the union ended, the former Russian Republic became a separate country, the Russian Federation, under the leadership of Boris N. Yeltsin.

The Russian Federation: In nine years as president of Russia (1991–2000), Yeltsin oversaw a chaotic transformation that ended the dominance of communism and brought irregular reforms in the economic, political, and social realms. Although the constitution of 1993 made the executive the dominant branch of government, Yeltsin struggled with the legislative branch over many issues. Economic reform was undermined by corruption and public suspicion as Russia nominally moved toward a free-market system. Judicial reform was piecemeal and ineffective. Relations with the West, which began the 1990s in close concert, soured somewhat over issues such as expansion of the North Atlantic Treaty Organization, Russia's ongoing conflicts with the Republic of Chechnya, and Russia's opposition to the United States-led war in Iraq in 2003. A new concentration of executive power began with the presidency of Vladimir V. Putin (elected in 2000), Yeltsin's handpicked successor who sought to restore Russia's regional power while maintaining relations with the West. Putin was reelected overwhelmingly in 2004. In the first six years of his presidency, political opposition became extremely fragmented, media independence lessened significantly, and Putin was able to shift the center of economic power from a group of independent entrepreneurs to government-controlled enterprises and cronies. Although repression of the media and nongovernmental organizations increasingly strained relations with the West, in 2006 Putin retained guarded support from Western governments and gained prestige by hosting a meeting of the G–8 nations.

GEOGRAPHY

Click to Enlarge Image

Location: Russia occupies much of easternmost Europe and northern Asia, stretching from Norway to the Pacific Ocean and from the Black Sea to the Arctic Ocean.

Size: With an area of 17,075,200 square kilometers (16,995,800 of which are land surface), Russia is the largest country in the world.

Land Boundaries: Russia's land boundaries extend 21,139 kilometers, bordering the following nations: Azerbaijan (284 kilometers), Belarus (959 kilometers), China (3,645 kilometers), Estonia (290 kilometers), Finland (1,313 kilometers), Georgia (723 kilometers), Kazakhstan (6,846 kilometers), the Democratic People's Republic of Korea (North Korea) (19 kilometers), Latvia (217 kilometers), Lithuania (227 kilometers), Mongolia (3,441 kilometers), Norway (167 kilometers), Poland (432 kilometers), and Ukraine (1,576 kilometers).

Disputed Territory: Russia has unresolved territorial disputes with Japan over the southernmost four Kuril Islands; with Ukraine over the maritime boundary in the Kerch Strait north of the Black Sea; and with other Caspian littoral states over control of offshore resources. In 2004 seabed treaties with Azerbaijan and Kazakhstan eliminated one issue in the Caspian region. Some border segments with Georgia, Estonia, and Latvia have not been accepted by both parties. In 2005 China and Russia ended a long dispute by agreeing to divide jurisdiction over river islands along their common border.

Length of Coastline: 37,653 kilometers, bordering the Arctic, Atlantic, and Pacific oceans.

Maritime Claims: Russia claims a 200-nautical-mile exclusive economic zone, a 12-nautical-mile territorial sea, and jurisdiction over the continental shelf to a 200-meter depth or to the depth of resource exploitation.

Topography: European Russia is dominated by a broad plain, with low hills west of the Ural Mountains. The Urals, considered the boundary between European and Asian Russia, stretch from the Arctic island of Novaya Zemlya to the border of Kazakhstan. East of the Urals is the vast West Siberian Plain, then the Central Siberian Plateau. East of the Central Siberian Plateau is the Lena Plateau. Russia's southern border with Mongolia and its entire Pacific coast are marked by mountain ranges. The border with China is defined by the Amur River valley. Siberia contains vast coniferous forests, to the north of which is a broad tundra zone extending to the Arctic Ocean. The southwestern border is marked by the uplands of the northern slope of the Caucasus Mountains. In Russia's southernmost extremity, flat, fertile steppe extends between its borders with Ukraine on the west and Kazakhstan on the east. About 10 percent of the country is swampland; about 45 percent is forested.

Principal Rivers: Russia's principal rivers are the Amur, Irtysh, Lena, Ob', and Volga. The Irtysh, Lena, and Ob' flow northward across Asian Russia into the Arctic Ocean. The Volga is the longest river in Europe. All of these rivers have complex systems of tributaries that collectively drain much of Russia's territory.

Climate: The climate of Russia's vast territory ranges from temperate to Arctic continental. European Russia receives some maritime climatic influence from the Baltic and Black seas and the Atlantic Ocean; from the Urals to the Far East, the climate is fully continental. The Pacific Ocean provides the southern Far East with warm, humid monsoon conditions. Winter weather varies from short-term and cold along the Black Sea to long-term and frigid in northern Siberia. Summer conditions range from warm on the steppes to cool along the Arctic coast. Much of Russia is covered by snow for six months of the year, and the weather often is harsh and unpredictable. In European Russia, the average annual temperature is 0° C; Moscow's average is 4° C. In Moscow the average midsummer high temperature is 23°, and the average midwinter high temperature is –9° C. The yearly average in southern Siberia is 0° C and in north-central Siberia –9° C. The Pacific port of Vladivostok averages 5° C. The precipitation in most areas is low to moderate. Mountains in the northwest receive as much as 2,000 millimeters annually, and points on the Pacific Coast receive as much as 1,000 millimeters.

Natural Resources: Russia possesses a vast variety of natural resources, many of which are located far from industrial processing centers. The fuel resources that supported development of industrial centers in European Russia have been depleted, necessitating reliance on coal, natural gas, and petroleum from Siberian deposits. However, Russia still has an estimated 6 percent of the world's oil deposits and one-third of the world's natural gas deposits, making it a major exporter of both commodities. In 2005 oil extraction reached a new post-Soviet high, placing Russia close to Saudi Arabia as the world's largest producer. Rich deposits of most industrially valuable metals, diamonds, and phosphates also are found in Russia.

Russia's northerly location limits available agricultural land, which is concentrated in the area between the Black and Caspian seas, along the borders of Ukraine and Kazakhstan, and in southern and western Siberia. Poor soil and short seasons restrict agricultural production in the European north to livestock. Erosion has depleted soil quality in many farming areas. Siberia contains nearly 50 percent of the world's coniferous forests, but Russia's forest management has declined sharply in recent years, and commercial clear-cutting is reducing the forest stock at a rapid rate. Coastal and river waters have supported an extensive fishing industry, which also is threatened by pollution and poor regulation.

Land Use: In 2005 some 7.2 percent of Russia's land was classified as arable, 45 percent was forested, and 0.1 percent was planted to permanent crops. In 2003 about 46,000 square kilometers were irrigated.

Environmental Factors: Largely because Soviet-era industrial, energy, and agricultural policies ignored environmental protection, many sectors of Russia are considered environmentally hazardous. Most major industrial centers have poor air and water quality, and air quality in all urban centers is substandard. The Caspian and Black seas, the Sea of Azov, the Volga River, and Lake Baikal are areas of severe water pollution. Industrial nodes in the Kola Peninsula, central Siberia, and the Urals emit especially large amounts of air pollutants. Persistent, large-scale pipeline leaks have saturated the soil in large areas of Western Siberia and Chechnya with oil. Rapidly increasing numbers of vehicles, using unleaded gas, exacerbate air pollution. Agricultural soil quality is reduced by erosion and overgrazing, and unrestricted harvesting reduces natural forests. Unsafe disposal of radioactive materials pollutes coastal water, rivers, and terrestrial areas. Russia's 12 operational RBMK-type nuclear reactors are considered unsafe; some reactors (with design modifications) are not scheduled for shutdown until after 2010. Official environmental protection has declined since the early 1990s, when the public briefly supported meaningful reversal of Soviet environmental practices. In 2000 the Putin government abolished Russia's Environmental Protection Committee (which earlier had lost its ministry status) and the Federal Forest Service. After substantial delay, in 2004 Russia ratified the Kyoto Protocol on greenhouse gases, making possible the enforcement of the protocol in signatory nations.

Time Zones: Russia's territory includes 11 time zones. Moscow is three hours ahead of Greenwich Mean Time.

SOCIETY

Population: In August 2006, Russia's population was an estimated 142.4 million, a decrease of 4.1 million since 1989. That total made Russia the seventh most populous country in the world. However, a long-term population decline of 600,000 per year is forecast, reducing the population to as little as 112 million by 2050. Of the 2006 total, 73 percent live in cities and towns and 27 percent in rural areas, a ratio that has remained stable since 1989. Some 89 million people (61 percent of the population) were of working age in 2002, but the working-age population was expected to decrease by as much as 15 percent during the ensuing 20 years. In 2004 the number of abortions (1.6 million) exceeded the number of live births (1.5 million), continuing a trend of the early 2000s.

About 1 million residents of Russia are citizens of other countries. In 2006 the estimated rate of net migration was 1.03 persons per 1,000 population, compared with a rate of 0.9 in 2004. Between 2002 and 2004, the rate had decreased by 55 percent. In 2005 net migration was 107,000, an increase of 7.5 percent over 2004.

Demography: In 2004 the average age was 37.7 years, an increase of three years since 1989, indicating a steadily aging population. In 2006 only 14 percent of the population was younger than 15 years of age, and 14 percent was older than 64. Life expectancy was 60.5 years for men, 74.1 for women—one of the largest life expectancy differentials by sex in the world. Some 53.7 percent of the population was female. The birthrate was 9.9 per 1,000 population; the death rate was 14.7 per 1,000 population. Infant mortality was 15.1 per 1,000 live births, and the average number of children born per woman of childbearing age was 1.3.

Ethnic Groups and Languages: According to the 2002 census, the largest ethnic groups were Russians (representing 80 percent of the total), Tatars, Ukrainians, Bashkirs, Chuvash, Chechens, and Armenians, each of which accounted for at least 1 million residents. The official language is Russian; approximately 100 other languages are spoken. Ethnic intolerance has increased steadily in the Russian population; in the early 2000s, more than 50 percent of respondents in polls consistently advocated strong restrictions or expulsion of ethnic minorities.

Religion: The official state religion is Russian Orthodoxy, which enjoys a privileged position with the government. About 75 million Russians belong to that faith, but fewer than half of that number are considered active worshippers. The fastest growing religion is Islam, professed by about 20 million, a much higher percentage of whom are considered active participants. Other religions are Roman Catholicism, 1.3 million; Judaism, between 400,000 and 550,000; and Jehovah's Witnesses, 131,000. Religious activity increased markedly following the collapse of communist rule in 1991, but restrictions have remained for certain groups. A 1997 law set requirements that religions be registered, putting unrecognized groups at a disadvantage. For example, all Muslim groups falling outside the government-sanctioned Spiritual Directorate of Muslims of Russia are repressed as potential terrorist organizations.

Education and Literacy: Russia traditionally has had a highly educated population. According to the 2002 census, 99.5 percent of the population above age 10 was literate. The constitution guarantees the right to free preschool, basic general, and secondary vocational education. Nine years of basic general education are compulsory, from age six until age 15. The first three years are considered primary, the remaining years secondary. After exclusive state operation of the education system in the Soviet era, many private education institutions appeared in the 1990s. In the early 2000s, incomplete curriculum reform has impeded training in new technical fields. Beginning in the 1990s, the teaching profession has suffered from low pay and loss of qualified individuals, and textbooks, computers, and laboratories have been in short supply. In the early 2000s, many private institutions of higher learning opened. By 2004 more than 1,000 public and private institutions were in operation, and 6.9 million students were enrolled in higher education programs in 2005. Unlike the Soviet period, about half of higher education students pay fees and/or entrance bribes. The education budget fell drastically in the 1990s, although the Putin administration has restored it somewhat since 2002. In 2004 some 4.9 percent of the national budget was allocated to education.

Health: Health care is free in principle, but in practice adequate treatment increasingly depends on wealth, and private health care is increasingly sought. Doctors generally are poorly trained and inadequately paid; most hospitals are in poor condition—many lack running water and sewerage—and waiting lists are long. There is a persistent shortage of nurses, specialized personnel, and medical supplies and equipment. Distribution of facilities and medical personnel is highly skewed in favor of urban areas, especially politically influential cities. Russia's high ratio of hospital beds to population—12.1 to 1,000 in 1998—is because outpatient care is not emphasized as much as in the West. In 2004 there were 4.9 doctors per 1,000 inhabitants.

The poor quality of air and water in many areas and the prevalence of heavy smoking and alcohol use (especially among men) exacerbate the overall poor health of the nation. Preventive health care is a low priority. The medical conditions most frequently causing death are cardiovascular disease (the cause of more than half of deaths), cancer, respiratory diseases, and diabetes. In the early 2000s, declining health care and housing standards led to increases in communicable diseases such as tuberculosis, diphtheria, and cholera. Among children, poor nutrition has increased the incidence of anemia, stomach ulcers, endocrine disorders, and iodine deficiency. The mortality rate for traffic accidents is nearly twice the rate in Western Europe, and in 2005 some 36,000 people died from alcohol abuse.

In 2006 Russia's Federal AIDS (acquired immune deficiency syndrome) Center reported 1.5 million confirmed cases of human immunodeficiency virus (HIV), 341,000 of which were officially registered. In 2005 Russia had the most rapid rate of increase in HIV cases outside sub-Saharan Africa. By that time, sexual activity had overtaken narcotics use as the main avenue of HIV transmission, and the trafficking of Russian women for the sex industry in Europe made Russia's high HIV rate an international concern. Poor health care in the prisons made them another major source of HIV-positive individuals. In 2006 the government allocated an estimated US$115 million to HIV and AIDS programs, but local administration and public education remained ineffective.

Responding to Russia's health crisis, in 2005 President Putin included health care in a list of five top national priorities and called for an increase of 85 percent in health-related allocations in the 2006 federal budget and additional increases in future budgets. Most of the 2006 money was to pay for increased wages for health professionals and facilities improvements.

Welfare: In the 1990s, economic transition and the end of Soviet-era public welfare forced more Russians into poverty as state social support programs failed to meet the social needs of a new economic system. Most enterprises provide an extensive social safety net for their workers, including maternity leave, child allowances, housing, paid vacations, and medical care. Worker pensions are funded by employers through a single social tax and by a direct assessment on self-employed workers and independent farmers. However, many workers are forced to postpone retirement because the post-Soviet pension system, which is Russia's largest expenditure for social welfare, has not been adequate to provide for retirees. When the decreasing ratio of active workers to pensioners threatened the system's viability, in 2002 Russia introduced a new system in which a portion of the mandatory pension payments of employers is invested in pension funds whose proceeds are earmarked for the pensions of workers born after 1967. Participation in private pension funds is expected to increase rapidly by 2010. Between 2002 and 2004, average monthly benefits increased from US$45 to US$58.

In 2005 a major welfare reform program began with a very unpopular monetization of privileges such as free transportation and medicine. Subsequently, monetization was made optional, and in

2006 less than half of recipients accepted cash compensation. In early 2006, about 52 million Russians were receiving some form of welfare. In 2006 officially 15 percent of the population fell below the minimum subsistence level. However, independent estimates were 25 percent or higher, and the incomes of 80 percent of Russians reportedly were falling. The geographical distribution of poverty was very uneven; in some regions, the rate was below 10 percent, whereas in others it reached 70 percent.

Government antipoverty measures have been undermined by ongoing high inflation. In 2006 Minister of Economics German Gref called for a fundamental overhaul of Russia's state welfare system. Most welfare agencies are run at the local or regional rather than the national level, and they suffer from inadequate funding and corruption. No agency ministers specifically to the homeless, whose number has grown since 1991. The Fund for Social Support, which maintains a number of social assistance programs, has suffered from corruption scandals. Private charities do not function as freely or as actively as in the West; in 2005 total charitable donations were estimated at US$1.5 billion. In an effort to stem Russia's demographic crisis, in 2006 the government doubled child support payments to US$55 per month and offered a one-time payment of US$9,200 to women who had a second child.

ECONOMY

Overview: Since 1991 Russia's economy has undergone major changes as a result of the rejection of the Soviet state planning system and the adoption of various elements of free-market commerce. The highly structured Soviet system, nominally following the standards of five-year plans, was succeeded by ambitious restructuring aimed at encouraging private enterprise. However, in the mid-1990s government privatization plans were undermined by corruption, which concentrated significant economic resources in the hands of a well-connected elite rather than effecting true redistribution. Large sectors of the state-owned enterprise system, especially those in energy, transportation, communications, and heavy industry, remained under government control, and by 2005 the state had re-nationalized about one-third of the private oil and gas sector. In a poll taken late in 2005, 47 percent of respondents favored a state-run economy, and only 16 percent advocated a free-market economy. Plans for extensive privatization in 2007 concentrated on firms in non-production spheres, agro-industry, and the defense industry. In 2005 an estimated 25 to 40 percent of the gross domestic product (GDP) derived from "informal" economic activity, and organized crime continued to play a significant role in many types of enterprise. In 2005 the richest 10 percent of the population accounted for 30 percent of Russia's income, and the poorest 10 percent accounted for 2 percent of the income. This distribution remained constant between 2004 and 2005. The disparity between average incomes in Russia's richest and poorest regions widened in 2005–6.

In the 1990s, the relative importance of the economic sectors changed significantly. Between 1991 and 2005, the share of the GDP derived from retail trade and services increased from 36 percent to nearly 58 percent, as the share of agriculture decreased from 14 percent to 5 percent. In the same period, the GDP contribution of industry dropped from nearly 50 percent to 37 percent. Large enterprises continue to dominate the economy to the detriment of small and medium-sized enterprises, which in 2005 contributed only 10 to 15 percent of GDP. The industrial sector is dominated by heavy industry, particularly fuels and energy (20 to 25 percent of output) and metallurgy (17 percent of output). High-technology and consumer goods production are minor constituents, and light industry contributes only 2 percent of total output. Throughout the early 2000s, raw materials exports have contributed a disproportionately high percentage to Russia's economic growth, and the reduction of this dependency has been a high priority for economic planners. The ongoing emigration of scientists, 25,000 of whom left between 1990 and 2005, threatens the technical base of the economy.

Gross Domestic Product (GDP): In the first five post-Soviet years (1992–96), Russia's GDP fell by an aggregate 37 percent. The indicator rose in 1997, then fell steeply as Russia suffered a major economic crisis. In 1999 the GDP began a six-year trend of expansion that continued in 2006. The major factors in this rise were rapidly expanding oil and gas sales, government tax reforms, and improved investor confidence. In 2004 Russia's GDP was US$657 billion (US$1.41 trillion in terms of purchasing power parity), an increase of 7.1 percent over the 2003 figure. At that point, GDP had increased by at least 4 percent every year since the economic crisis of 1998. In 2005 GDP increased by 6.4 percent to US$741 billion. The official government forecast for 2006 was a 6.6 percent increase; long-term forecasts called for increases of 6 percent in 2007, 5.8 percent in 2008, and 5.9 percent in 2009, subject to oil and gas price trends. Per capita GDP increased in 2005 by 6.8 percent, to US$5,393, or US$11,100 in terms of purchasing power parity. In 2005 the services sector contributed 57.5 percent to GDP, the industrial sector 37.1 percent, and the agricultural sector 5.4 percent. Regional contributions to GDP vary sharply; in 2005 the city of Moscow contributed 20 percent and the oil-rich province of Tyumen' added 13 percent, while 72 of Russia's other 87 jurisdictions made a collective contribution of 37 percent.

Federal Budget: From 2000 through 2005, Russia's federal budget showed surpluses each year. Tax revenues tripled between 1999 and 2002. Following the tax reform of 2001, which established a flat 13 percent income tax rate, income tax revenues increased annually through the early 2000s. The 2001 reform also reduced the corporate tax rate from 35 percent to 24 percent, and in 2004 the value-added tax was reduced from 20 percent to 18 percent. Although some 32 percent more income tax money was collected in 2005 than in 2004 and the Federal Taxation Service campaigned to eradicate unreported salaries, in 2006 an estimated one-third of wage payments still were unrecorded. Tax revenues for 2005 were US$153 billion. In 2005 the budget showed a surplus of US$51.1 billion, based on revenues of US$176.7 billion and expenditures of US$125.6 billion. The budget for 2006 called for US$197 billion in revenues and US$144 billion in expenditures, a surplus of US$53 billion. In the first eight months of the year, the actual budget surplus was US$56 billion. In 2006 the government's Stabilization Fund, established as a hedge against future decreases in oil revenue, had about US$27 billion. The preliminary 2007 budget called for US$260 billion in revenues (based on further rises in oil prices) and US$211 in expenditures. By 2005 the failure to use budget surpluses efficiently had become a controversial issue in the government.

Inflation: In the first half of the 1990s, hyperinflation was a major economic problem, as the annual rate reached 2,500 percent in 1992. After price stabilization brought the inflation rate down to 11 percent in 1997, the financial collapse of 1998 and subsequent currency devaluation raised inflation that year to 84.5 percent. Since that time, inflationary pressure has remained a sensitive policy issue, although rates have receded significantly. Stimulated by high costs for fuel and manufacturing inputs, the official rate for 2004 was 11.7 percent, exceeding the government target of 10 percent. The rate for 2005 was 11 percent. In the first eight months of 2006, prices increased by 7.1 percent, somewhat less than the increase in the same period of 2005. The official target for 2007 was 7 percent.

Agriculture: Russia's agricultural potential, limited by climatic and soil factors to 32 percent of the country's land area, has been further depleted by policies such as overly intensive farming, overuse of chemicals, and inappropriate crop choice. In the post-Soviet era, failure to effectively convert inefficient collective farms to private ownership has further hampered production. Limited sale of agricultural land was approved only in 2002 and, because of the political sensitivity of the issue, as of 2006 comprehensive land reform legislation still had not been passed. In the 1990s, Russia's agricultural production fell sharply. After declines of more than 50 percent in every major crop, output began to increase somewhat in 1999. Between 2003 and 2005, the average annual increase was 3 percent. However, farm infrastructure has declined sharply, and farmers lack funds to purchase key inputs. Federal and subnational jurisdictions still subsidize agriculture heavily instead of developing incentives for independent entrepreneurship. In 2005 grain remained the largest crop, occupying more than 50 percent of cultivated land. Other key crops were sugar beets, sunflower seed, and vegetables. The main livestock outputs were cow's milk, beef and veal, eggs, and pork.

Forestry: About 45 percent of Russia's land is covered by forests. Russia, which has about one-quarter of the world's forest resources, is a major exporter of timber. However, wasteful timber policies have caused the industry to move steadily eastward into Siberia, and the per-hectare output of Russia's forests is far behind outputs elsewhere. Insects, forest fires, and industrial pollution have reduced stands of timber, and the output of the domestic timber industry declined in the late 1990s and early 2000s. However, in the same period exploitation by foreign companies and criminal organizations in Siberia has expanded rapidly without adequate licensing and control. The Federal Forestry Agency announced a national plan against poaching in 2006. Adoption of a new forestry code to address these problems, originally scheduled for 2005, was delayed again in 2006. In 2005 Russia exported 50 million cubic meters of timber products, about one-quarter of its total output. China received about 40 percent of that amount.

Fishing: In 1991 the Soviet Union was the world's fourth largest producer of fish. Production has declined steadily since that time because of inefficient privatization of the industry and pollution in certain fishing areas. Although by 2002 Russia had fallen to eighth in the world in fishing output, the export share of the total catch increased to 80 percent in 2001. In 2004 the fishing output totaled 3,250 tons, nearly all of which was caught rather than raised by aquaculture, compared with 3,720 tons in 2001. The yield from Pacific fisheries, a primary source, has been restricted by extensive poaching in Russia's Far East.

Mining and Minerals: Russia's diverse mineral resources have given many of its products a strong position in world markets. Of particular economic importance are diamonds, of which in 2006 Russia accounted for one-quarter of world production; nickel (one-third); cobalt (20 percent); platinum (40 percent); and aluminum (12 percent). The economic slump of the early 1990s caused overall production to decrease and the proportion of exports to increase. The coal industry, forced by depleted resources to more northerly and less economical sites, remains a key industry in some regions but requires large-scale restructuring. Russia still is second only to the United States in coal reserves, however. The oil and gas industries, among the largest in the world, provide key export commodities, although transport within the country and conflicts over the energy sector's structure have provided obstacles. The oil industry underwent a major restructuring in 2003–4. The government has delayed restructuring the heavily subsidized coal sector.

Industry and Manufacturing: After 1991 Russia's industrial sector continued to rely heavily on defense industries and heavy manufacturing, despite an evident need for diversification. At the end of the Soviet era, Russia's manufacturing infrastructure was decaying and energy-intensive, although it produced (and continues to produce) a wide range of chemical, metallurgical, and machine-building products, communications and transportation equipment, and ships. Lacking the subsidies and captive markets of the Soviet era, the industrial sector in the 1990s was not internationally competitive. Shortages of investment and human capital were other disadvantages leading to a drastic decrease in production, which by 1998 was only 45 percent of the 1990 level. Especially hard-hit in this period were the consumer goods and metallurgy industries. Light industry, of which textiles is the main component, declined because of its outdated infrastructure and inability to compete on the world market. In 2005 the majority of heavy and light manufacturing categories suffered significant declines in growth rates. Between 2004 and 2005, the overall growth rate of manufacturing decreased from 6.1 percent to 5.7 percent. The food-processing industry showed the greatest growth in productivity in that period.

After a sharp drop in the 1990s, production in the defense sector increased significantly beginning in 1999; restructuring of that chronically obsolete sector has concentrated on high-technology items and products for civilian application. Plans call for the latter outputs to account for 70 percent of the defense sector's production by 2015. Increased foreign sales, particularly to China and India, and some increases in domestic military spending have spurred growth. In 2005 military exports were estimated at US$6 billion.

Energy: Russia possesses abundant resources for energy production, making it a net exporter of electric power and the largest producer of energy in the world. Increasingly, Russia has used this position as a geopolitical lever to enhance its influence in the states of the former Soviet Union and to influence world energy prices. In 2006 the oil and gas industry contributed as much as 25 percent of gross domestic product, and oil accounted for 35 percent of Russia's exports.

Electric power stations utilize a variety of fuels and energy sources: petroleum, coal, and natural gas (together providing 66.3 percent of the total); hydroelectric power (17.2 percent); and nuclear power (16.4 percent). Plans call for substantial increases in hydroelectric production in the Far East and five new reactors at the 10 existing nuclear plants. In 2006 the system's total generating capacity was about 210 gigawatts. The national electric power grid is divided into seven regional systems, all but one of which is fed from a state-controlled monopoly, the Unified Energy System. Energy supply problems include wasteful practices in all phases of production and supply; long distances between sites of fuel supply and power generation and between sites of power generation and consumption; a distribution infrastructure suffering from long-term

11

neglect; a dangerously outmoded nuclear power infrastructure; and ownership uncertainty and tax pressure on key oil and gas enterprises.

A 2003 law aimed to restructure the energy sector substantially, including extensive privatization of energy provision and elimination of the Unified Energy System. Although major reform of the energy industry was not expected until after the 2008 presidential election, in 2006 plans called for encouraging foreign investment in generating infrastructure. In the 1990s and the early 2000s, the oil and gas industries relied largely on existing deposits and infrastructure. As of 2006, they had built no new refineries for 15 years, and geological exploration ceased entirely for several years. Extraction efficiency from existing deposits is extremely low. The dominant player in the fuels sector is the Gazprom company, which controls natural gas production, owns the gas pipeline system, and has diversified into transport and gas processing as well as telecommunications. Gazprom, in which the state holds majority ownership, controls an estimated 30 percent of the world's natural gas reserves. The extensive Shtokman natural gas field in the Barents Sea is expected to be productive for as much as 50 years, but Russia has delayed exploitation to coincide with increased world demand for liquefied natural gas. Yukos, until 2004 Russia's largest oil company, lost most of its assets during the government's campaign against its president, Mikhail Khodorkovskiy. At that point, an estimated 30 percent of oil output came from state companies. The largest such company, Lukoil, is responsible for 18 percent of production.

Services: Russia's services sector has expanded rapidly in the post-Soviet era, contributing 57.5 percent of gross domestic product (GDP) in 2005. Financial services have expanded especially fast during that period. Between 2002 and 2006, total bank deposits increased sixfold. Banking remains highly concentrated and dominated by the state-run Sberbank, although by 2005 Sberbank's share of total savings had decreased from the 2003 level of 70 percent to 55 percent. Bank reform has not yet expanded the basic services offered. A deposit insurance system came into full operation in 2005. In 2006 protectionist laws continued to restrict severely the activity of foreign banks in Russia.

Although stock trading grew rapidly in the late 1990s, in the years following the financial crisis of 1998 stock sales were not an important source of investment funds for Russian enterprises. However, between 2004 and early 2006 stock capitalization increased from 50 percent to 80 percent of GDP as the market grew rapidly. The insurance industry also grew rapidly in the 1990s, but in the early 2000s it occupied a substantially less significant position than in Western economies, and foreign participation has been limited by restrictive laws. In 2005 about 1,000 insurance companies were operating, but the 50 largest held 70 percent of policy value.

In the post-Soviet era, retail services have prospered, expanding annually in value by 9.5 percent between 2000 and 2002. However, although many retail companies are established in the major cities, most of Russia lacks adequate retail outlets. Even Moscow, the center of retail activity, has much less activity than comparable capitals. Outside Moscow and St. Petersburg, outdoor markets are the predominant type of retail outlet. In 2005 retail sales totaled US$245 billion, about 32 percent of GDP.

The tourism industry has grown significantly since the mid-1990s, although activity is concentrated in large cities where Western-owned hotels predominate. Less expensive accommodations have developed slowly. In 2002 a government tourism development plan aimed at easing tourist access and increasing promotion and investment in the industry. In 2004 about 23 million tourists visited Russia, and tourism contributed an estimated 9 percent of GDP. However, beginning in 2004 the introduction of a visa regime by new European Union member countries in Eastern Europe reduced tourist visits from those countries. (About 1 million tourists had come from Poland in 2003.) The tourist market in China expanded to about 1 million in 2005 and was expected to increase further, and domestic tourist travel increased steadily in the early 2000s. An estimated 5 million people work in the tourism industry.

Labor: Russia's labor force generally is considered well-educated and skilled, although its strengths increasingly are mismatched to the needs of the national economy. In 2005 Russia's active labor force was estimated at 74.2 million individuals. In 2004 the government estimated that the number of individuals of working age, 89 million in 2002, would decrease by some 10 million by 2016. Because the indigenous labor force is shrinking by as much as 1 million workers per year, the government considers long-term expansion of the immigrant labor force necessary to sustain economic growth. However, that strategy has encountered substantial resistance in Russian society. In the early 2000s, non-Russian ethnic groups gained control of some sectors. For example, Azeris controlled wholesale fruit and vegetable sales in Moscow and other cities.

In 2005 some 68.3 percent of workers were employed in services, 21.4 percent in industry, and 10.3 percent in agriculture. The official unemployment rate was 7.6 percent, although because of incomplete registration and substantial underemployment the actual figure was believed to be considerably higher. Unemployment, which is highest among women and young people, is distributed unevenly throughout the country: in 2003 some 1.3 percent of the work force in Moscow was unemployed, while the republics of Kalmykia and Tyva, heavily dependent on failing industries, reported unemployment rates of more than 21 percent. In 2006 the minimum wage, which at its 2004 level of US$20 per month was estimated to cover only 22 percent of basic living costs, was raised to US$40 per month. In 2006 average wages rose by 23 percent, less than the average increase in the early 2000s, but the average wages of civil service workers increased by one-third.

Foreign Economic Relations: The improvement of Russia's foreign trade and foreign investment positions has been a central policy of the Putin administration. In 2005 Russia took major steps toward its most important foreign trade goal, membership in the World Trade Organization (WTO). However, in the fall of 2006 the United States continued to block Russia's admission despite intensive negotiations. Among critical issues in the U.S. position were copyright piracy in Russia and restrictions on U.S. exports to Russia.

In 2005 a new agreement extended cooperation with the European Union (EU) in a wide variety of economic and security areas and committed the EU to supporting Russia's WTO membership. For the European side, a vital motivation for supporting Russia's membership was minimizing the price of Russian gas and oil upon which EU nations depend. In the post-Soviet era, Russia has maintained strong trade relationships with several states of the Commonwealth of

Independent States (CIS), especially Belarus, Ukraine, and Kazakhstan. By 2005, however, trade with CIS nations had declined steadily to less than 15 percent of the total as trade with the countries of the EU increased to more than 50 percent of the total, based on increasingly favorable conditions. During the entire post-Soviet era, Germany has been Russia's highest-volume partner in both imports and exports, accounting for 13.4 percent of imports and 8.0 percent of exports in 2005. China also accounts for at least 5 percent of both imports and exports. In 2005 trade between China and Russia increased by 37 percent to US$29 billion. Italy, the Netherlands, Turkey, and Ukraine were Russia's other largest export customers in 2005, and Finland, Italy, Japan, and Ukraine were its other largest sources of imports.

In the early 2000s, Russia increasingly used demand for its foreign hydrocarbons as a political lever. In 2006 Russia raised gas prices for Ukraine, whose democratic government Russia disfavored, by about 100 percent, and a new trans-Baltic pipeline will deprive Ukraine and Poland, another state at odds with Russia, of fees for overland transit of Russian oil to Europe. The scheduled opening of a trans-Siberian oil pipeline in 2008 would significantly re-orient Russia's oil exports toward Asia, which has been identified as Russia's next great fuel market. China and India are the chief customers of Russia's defense industry.

Trade Balance: Devaluation of the ruble in 1998 improved Russia's export situation and began an annual trend of trade surpluses. In 2005 exports were valued at US$245 billion, led by petroleum products and natural gas, which accounted for 63 percent of the total. Imports were valued at US$125 billion, led by machinery and equipment, food and agricultural products, and chemicals.

Balance of Payments: In 2004 all items in Russia's current account except merchandise trade were in deficit, but the overall current account balance was US$60.1 billion, and the overall balance of payments was US$46.6 billion. In 2005 the same conditions yielded a current account balance of US$84.3 billion and an overall balance of US$65.6 billion. Large-scale capital outflow, a major problem in the post-Soviet era, continued to affect the balance of payments in 2005, totaling a negative US$53 billion compared with the 2004 figure of US$34 billion. Nearly half of the 2005 figure was illegal capital flight, a significantly smaller proportion than in 2004. In 2004 the balance of net investment income was negative US$12.2 billion, while foreign direct investment showed a balance of US$11.7 billion. In early 2006, Russia's international reserves had increased to US$196 billion.

External Debt: In 1991 Russia assumed the Soviet Union's outstanding debt of US$67.5 billion, but by 1997 additional borrowing had doubled that figure, and international creditors rescheduled the debt several times between 1995 and 2001. Since 2001, creditors have increased pressure for repayment because of Russia's favorable trade balance and increasing foreign-exchange reserves. At the end of 2004, the external debt totaled US$197.4 billion, but in 2005 and 2006 Russia used its oil-fed Stabilization Fund to repay substantial amounts to the International Monetary Fund and the Paris Club of international lenders.

Foreign Investment: Compared with the size of Russia's economy, foreign investment levels have remained very low throughout the post-Soviet era. The reasons for this have been an unfavorable tax system, corruption, the lack of production-sharing agreements in the fuel sector, and overall economic uncertainty. The United States has been the largest foreign investor in Russia, accounting for about one-third of the investment total between 1991 and 2000. A significant development in 2003 was British Petroleum's decision to invest US$6.7 billion in Russia's petroleum industry. Russia's government policy generally has prevented foreign interests from gaining significant shares of the energy industries. According to 2006 legislation, foreign firms could obtain only minority ownership of any energy project deemed "strategic." In 2006 laws preventing foreign banks from opening branches in Russia remained a significant hindrance to Russia's accession to the World Trade Organization. Total foreign investment for 2004 was US$40.5 billion, with consumer goods and services and construction receiving the largest shares among the economic sectors. In 2005 the figure rose to US$56 billion, with the heaviest investments coming from Luxembourg, Cyprus, the Netherlands, Germany, Britain, the United States, and France. Foreign direct investment for 2005 was US$16.7 billion. Increases of 42 percent in overall investment and 44 percent in foreign direct investment, compared with the same period in 2005, were reported in the first half of 2006.

Currency and Exchange Rate: Russia's currency is the ruble. Between 2000 and 2004, the value of the ruble remained steady at around 31 per U.S. dollar. In mid-October 2006, the rate was nearly 27 rubles per US$1. In mid-2006, the Duma passed legislation that would make the ruble fully convertible.

Fiscal Year: Russia's fiscal year is the calendar year.

TRANSPORTATION AND TELECOMMUNICATIONS

Overview: In the post-Soviet era, Russia's transportation infrastructure has continued the process of deterioration that began in the last years of Soviet governance. The systems also suffer from a Soviet administrative design ill-suited to a market economy: modes of transportation are vertically integrated, placing control of all aspects, from equipment production to station management, under the same authority. That handicap, together with the long distances covered by roads and railroads, adverse climatic conditions, and the stress of the post-Soviet transition, places Russia in need of massive overhauls in all aspects of its transportation system. Modes of ground transport have dominated passenger traffic. According to a 2006 poll, 82 percent of Russians have traveled by motor vehicle, 64 percent by railroad, and 15 percent by air.

Roads: In 2005 Russia had 897,000 kilometers of roads, 762,000 of which were paved but none of which could be classified as a Western-style trunk highway. An estimated 40 percent of rural villages are not connected to a paved road. In 1999 an estimated 43 percent of federal roads (which account for 46,000 kilometers and half of the country's trucking volume) did not meet minimum quality standards because of broken surfaces, poor marking, and poor lighting. Road conditions are a major factor in Russia's very high rate of traffic casualties. The road crisis is exacerbated by steady increases in vehicle volume. The Roads of Russia program, established in 1998, has aimed at large-scale restructuring, including conversion of some federal roads into privatized toll roads. In 2004 the program laid out road building plans through 2025, with early phases concentrated around Moscow. However, only 2,000 kilometers of new roads were built in

2005. A US$2.6 billion investment fund established in 2006 will target infrastructure improvement and projects around Moscow and St. Petersburg.

Railroads: Railroads also are a vital economic link, particularly important for hauling coal, coke, ferrous metals, ores, chemicals, fertilizers, grain, and timber products. Largely because of increasingly poor long-distance road conditions, between 1992 and 2004 the share of total freight haulage by the railroads increased from 34 percent to 43 percent, and in 2005 they carried 80 percent of Russia's non-pipeline traffic. Rail transport of oil to seaports increased significantly in the early 2000s. The railroads also accounted for 38 percent of passenger transport. In 2005 Russia had 87,000 kilometers of rail line, nearly all of which was broad gauge, including 46 percent electrified. An additional 30,000 kilometers of rail line served specific industries. Although the government has recognized the need to restructure this system to keep it competitive with the improving road system, Russia's railroads have remained a state monopoly. The system is divided into 17 regional railroads, which have a contractual relationship with the Ministry of Railways. A restructuring plan adopted in 2001 calls for partial privatization between 2006 and 2010, with the creation of separate state enterprises for constituent services as an intermediate step. Priority projects are improved telecommunications and traffic control and modernization of rolling stock. As of 2005, the plan had made little progress, however. In 2005 six cities had underground rail lines: Moscow, Nizhniy Novgorod, Novosibirsk, St. Petersburg, Samara, and Yekaterinburg.

Ports: The breakup of the Soviet Union deprived Russia of 51 of the 92 marine ports to which it had access prior to 1991, necessitating reliance on other former Soviet countries for a large share of its seagoing commerce. Remaining Russian port capacity is not sufficient for the current level of foreign trade. In 2005 some 43 ports were in operation. The most important ports are St. Petersburg and Kaliningrad on the Baltic Sea, Novorossiysk and Sochi on the Black Sea, and Magadan, Nakhodka, Vladivostok, and Petropavlovsk on the Pacific Ocean. Two major ports above the Arctic Circle, Murmansk and Arkhangel'sk, are closed by ice part of each year. The Pacific ports are located far from European industrial and population centers. Demand far exceeds capacity at Novorossiysk, the main Black Sea port. Much infrastructure such as port cranes and loading machines is in poor condition and does not meet current international standards. Major deficiencies exist in freight forwarding systems, cargo processing terminals, integration of land and sea transport services, computerization of cargo flow, and cargo processing services. Government programs to improve port capacity have come under particular pressure from the oil industry's need for expanded port capacity, and that industry largely determines port development policy. A new oil terminal opened at Primorsk near St. Petersburg in 2001. Plans call for a new oil port at Perevoznaya Bay on the Sea of Japan as a Pacific terminus of the trans-Siberian pipeline scheduled for completion after 2008. Other port expansion programs have been delayed because of funding problems. In 2005 Russia's merchant marine had 1,199 ships with a gross registered tonnage of more than 1,000.

Inland Waterways: Russia has 102,000 kilometers of inland water routes. A system totaling 72,000 kilometers in European Russia links the Baltic, Black, and Caspian seas and the Arctic Ocean. Some 60,400 kilometers of the system have night navigation capability, and 16,900 kilometers are man-made navigation routes. The main European waterway is the Volga-Don system, which connects the major river ports of Nizhniy Novgorod, Kazan', Samara, Saratov,

Volgograd, Astrakhan', and Rostov with the Caspian Sea and the Black Sea and leads northward via canals to link with the Baltic Sea at St. Petersburg. The system links the Don and Volga rivers by the 60-kilometer Volga-Don Canal. Expansion of commerce on inland waterways has been hindered by shallow water and weather conditions. The Volga-Don Canal is closed for several months in winter.

Civil Aviation and Airports: Air travel decreased sharply in the 1990s; in 2001 passenger kilometers were less than 40 percent of the 1990 total. Passenger numbers recovered gradually in the early 2000s, increasing by 4 percent between 2004 and 2005 to about 35 million. However, in 2006 most domestically produced airliners had been in service for more than 20 years, as the aviation industry's output remained very low and funds for replacement were lacking. Safety concerns about the aging fleet accelerated in 2005–6 as crashes increased significantly. Although plans call for streamlining the Russian airline industry under a single United Aircraft Building Corporation, foreign builders Airbus and Boeing are expected to provide most of Russia's new airliners in the ensuing decade, further damaging the domestic industry. Despite losing its monopoly, Aeroflot remained the largest domestic carrier in 2005. Its 90 planes made flights to 54 countries from the hub city, Moscow, accounting for about 50 percent of Russia's air passenger kilometers. However, in 2005 foreign carriers increased their passengers by 12 percent, compared with a 2 percent increase by domestic lines. In 2006 Russia had 616 airports with paved runways, 51 of which had runways longer than 3,000 meters and 198, runways between 2,500 and 3,000 meters. Major international airports are located in Moscow, St. Petersburg, Rostov, Yekaterinburg, Novorossiysk, Krasnoyarsk, Irkutsk, Khabarovsk, and Magadan. In 2006 some 52 heliports also were in operation.

Pipelines: Because of the vital role of oil and natural gas in the national economy and the need to move those commodities over long distances, pipelines occupy a critical position in the national transportation system. The system includes 46,800 kilometers of trunk pipelines, 395 oil pumping stations, and 868 storage facilities. In 2005 the overall pipeline system included 150,007 kilometers for natural gas, 75,539 kilometers for oil, 13,771 kilometers for refined products, and 122 kilometers for gas condensate. The state-owned Transneft' company has monopoly control of that system, although the government has proposed privatization of some parts of the pipeline infrastructure. Transneft' is divided into several regional trunk-line operating companies. Several major new pipeline projects have been proposed to expedite transport to critical ports such as St. Petersburg, Murmansk, and Novorossiysk, relieving overloaded lines designated for export. The condition of the pipeline infrastructure has declined significantly in recent years; in many areas, maintenance is complicated by permafrost and climatic conditions. Modernization and expansion have been hindered by the monopoly positions of Transneft' and Gazprom. A new, 4,000-kilometer trans-Siberian oil pipeline was scheduled to begin deliveries to China and the Pacific in 2008 but has been delayed, and a planned Northern European line would bypass Poland and Ukraine to increase Russia's share of the West European natural gas market. In 2006 Russia agreed with Bulgaria and Greece to expedite construction of a natural gas line connecting Russia's Black Sea terminal Novorossiysk with Alexandroupolis on the Mediterranean Sea via Burgas.

Telecommunications: In the 1990s, Russia's telephone system underwent a major transition, as more than 1,000 companies gained licenses to provide services. The number of private lines increased sharply during that period, although long waiting periods remained the norm. The government's goal is to add 50 million land lines by 2010. Major developments in recent years include increased access to digital lines (mainly in urban centers) and major infrastructural improvements. However, the demand for main line service remains unmet, and service outside urban centers is inadequate. With extensive foreign investment, substantial growth occurred between 2003 and 2005, increasing the ratio of land lines per 1,000 inhabitants from 24.3 to 29.5. Digital trunk lines connect St. Petersburg on the Baltic with Khabarovsk in the Far East and Moscow with Novorossiysk on the Black Sea. Some 60 regional capitals offer modern digital systems, but in 2004 an estimated 54,000 rural communities lacked telephone service entirely. Driven by slow installation of conventional lines, cellular phone use has increased dramatically since 2000. Between 2002 and 2003, the number of cellular subscribers doubled to 36 million; by 2005 it had reached 120 million, and mobile telephones accounted for 43 percent of all communications services. In 2005 an estimated 60 percent of Russians used cellular phones: 72 percent of the urban population and 47 percent of the rural population. At the insistence of security agencies and the military, the government has postponed privatization of Svyazinvest, the state holding company that controls the long-distance monopoly Rostelkom and the 89 largest regional telephone companies.

Partly because of difficulties with the telecommunications infrastructure, Internet use has grown more slowly in Russia than elsewhere. The scarcity of home computers and high fees have been other obstacles. After a period of rapid growth of Internet use, in 2006 the number of users was estimated at 24 million; growth has been particularly dramatic in urban centers, especially Moscow, Irkutsk, Krasnodar, Nizhniy Novgorod, Novosibirsk, Vladivostok, and Yekaterinburg. The government has provided 10,000 public terminals in most regions. Corporate accounts make up about two-thirds of Internet use, and e-commerce has not expanded rapidly.

GOVERNMENT AND POLITICS

Overview: Russia is a democratic federation of 89 subnational jurisdictions, classified as republics, oblasts (provinces), autonomous oblasts, autonomous regions, and territories. At the national level, the constitution of 1993 calls for three branches of government—the executive, legislative, and judiciary—but it does not stipulate equal powers for each. In that system, the president of Russia has formidable powers as head of the armed forces and the Security Council. Those powers include the authority to appoint a wide variety of government officials without effective oversight or check. The houses of the bicameral legislative branch have offered only weak opposition because of their constitutional position and because effective opposition parties do not exist. The judiciary, a rubber-stamp branch of government under the Soviet system, has moved only slowly to assert an independent authority. President Vladimir Putin has used this structure to enhance the power of his office and dominate the government.

Executive Branch: The president, who is the head of state, serves a maximum of two four-year terms. However, in 2006, midway in the second term of Vladimir Putin, public opinion favored amending the constitution to allow him to seek a third term. The president appoints the prime minister (who is head of government), the head of the Central Bank of Russia, and the chairman of the highest judicial body, the Constitutional Court. Those nominations require confirmation by the State Duma, the lower house of parliament (the Federal Assembly), although the president may dissolve the Duma if it fails three times to confirm a nominee for prime minister. Several other top-level presidential nominations, however, require no approval from the legislative branch. The president also issues decrees that go into effect without the parliament's approval. Putin, who was elected in 2000 and reelected in 2004, has further improved his position by introducing changes that limit the power of the two houses of the Federal Assembly and through the plurality of his party in the Duma. There is no vice president; if the president is incapacitated, the prime minister succeeds him until a new election is held.

In 2006 the government, headed by Prime Minister Mikhail Fradkov, included 16 ministries, some of which are important policy-making centers. The three "power ministries"—Internal Affairs, Defense, and the Federal Security Service, which has ministerial status—are concerned with domestic and international security. The Ministry of Finance is the center of national economic policy making, and since 2000 the Ministry for Economic Development and Trade, which merged several Soviet-era ministries, has assumed a powerful economic policy position under German Gref. On many issues, the last two ministries are considered a counterweight to the "power ministries." Also included at "cabinet level" are the director of the Foreign Intelligence Service, the chairman of the Central Bank of Russia, and the procurator general, who is the chief prosecutor. Several powerful political "clans," tacitly united under the Putin administration, are expected to vie for power when Putin leaves office.

In late 2005, Putin authorized the 126-member Public Chamber, a new body designed to streamline public input into legislation and government policy. The appointive membership of the chamber includes accomplished individuals in a variety of civic, academic, and social fields. In its first year of existence, the chamber's 17 specialized committees intervened in several major policy areas.

Legislative Branch: The Federal Assembly is divided into two houses, the Federation Council (178 members) and the State Duma (450 members). Members of both houses serve four-year terms. The houses have differing responsibilities; the Duma has the more powerful role of primary consideration of all legislation. Although the Federation Council has the power to review and force compromise on legislation, in practice its role has been primarily as a consultative and reviewing body. In the 1990s, the Federation Council was made up of the heads of government and the legislative leaders of the 89 subnational jurisdictions into which Russia is divided. In 2000 Putin increased his control of the Federation Council by replacing ex-officio membership with a process of appointment by the president. The Duma can vote no-confidence in a sitting government, but the president can ignore the vote and dissolve the Duma if a second such vote is taken within three months. Changes in the constitution require a two-thirds vote in the Duma. The Duma elections of December 2003 gave a strong plurality (222 seats) to Putin's United Russia Party, which gained three times as many votes as the second-place Communist Party of the Russian Federation. Between that election and mid-2006, United Russia gained 87 seats as delegates switched party allegiance. In 2006 United Russia had 309 seats; the Communist Party, 45 seats; the Liberal Democratic Party of Russia, 35 seats; the Motherland bloc of regional parties, 29 seats; and the People's Party, 12 seats. Independents held 18 seats, and two seats were vacant. Some 45 members of the Duma and six of the Federation Council were women.

Judicial Branch: The judicial branch has moved very slowly toward an independent role in the post-Soviet era. The federal judicial institutions are the Constitutional Court, the Supreme Court, and the Superior Court for Arbitration. Judges of those courts serve lifetime terms. All federal judges are appointed by the Federation Council on the recommendation of the president. The 19-member Constitutional Court passes judgments on compliance with federal law and the constitution and settles jurisdictional disputes between state bodies. The 23-member Supreme Court rules on matters of civil, criminal, and administrative law. It is the final stage of the appeals system, which begins with local courts of general jurisdiction and includes district and regional courts. The specialty of the Superior Court for Arbitration is settling commercial disputes.

Administrative Divisions: Russia is divided into 89 subnational jurisdictions, each of which has two representatives in the Federation Council. However, those jurisdictions vary widely in size, composition, and nomenclature. They include 21 republics, 49 oblasts (provinces), six territories, 10 autonomous regions, one autonomous oblast, and two cities (Moscow and St. Petersburg) with separate oblast status. The autonomous regions and the autonomous oblast are parts of larger subnational jurisdictions. In a first step toward overcoming the complexity of this system, in 2000 all of Russia was divided into seven federal districts: Central, Far East, North Caucasus, Northwest, Siberia, Urals, and Volga. Within the 89 jurisdictions, the next-largest jurisdictional level is the *rayon*, which is approximately equivalent to a county in the United States.

Provincial and Local Government: The chief executive of all 89 jurisdictions is the governor. In December 2004, the selection method of governors was changed, increasing the power of the national executive over subnational governments. Instead of direct popular election in the jurisdiction, governors now are nominated by the president, then appointed by the jurisdiction's legislature. The legislature can reject a nominee, but after three rejections the president can dissolve the legislature. In 2005 all of President Putin's more than 30 nominees were approved immediately by the respective legislatures. The seven federal districts have governors who are appointed by the president. In 2006 a law substantially increased the oversight powers of regional governors over city mayors, reducing local governmental powers. A Law on Self-Government, expected to be finalized in 2009, is likely to result in interim reform creating large numbers of new municipalities, revising the present municipal government structure, and increasing the budgetary autonomy of all local jurisdictions. Implementation of some parts of the law began in 2004.

Judicial and Legal System: Civil and criminal cases are heard by courts of general jurisdiction, which are subordinate to the Supreme Court and function at district, regional, and national levels, with appeals possible to the next higher level. The chief legal representative of the state, the procurator general, is nominated by the president and approved by the Federation Council. The procurator general appoints equivalent officers for the lower jurisdictions. Military courts are included in this system. A second system is the arbitration or commercial courts, which hear business-related cases under the national Supreme Court of Arbitration. In 2006 a public justice system of about 500 courts went into operation to resolve certain commercial disputes otherwise heard by conventional courts. In all but two subnational jurisdictions, justices of the peace handle minor criminal cases and some civil cases, sometimes assuming as much as half the judicial caseload of the jurisdiction. Some of Russia's subnational jurisdictions have constitutional courts, which form the third court system under the authority of the national Constitutional Court.

Although Russia has committed itself to thorough reform of the rubber-stamp Soviet judicial system, progress in that direction has been slow. Federal judges are nominated by assemblies of judges and approved by the president. The Ministry of Justice administers the judicial system, naming judges and establishing courts below the federal level. However, in the 1990s many judges remained from the Soviet system, and the judiciary became a roadblock for reform programs such as privatization and improved human rights. The independence and professionalism of judges have been damaged by the minimal pay they have received, and funding of the judicial system has been problematic. Although salaries had increased substantially by 2005, bribery of judges remains a frequent practice.

A new Criminal Procedure Code went into effect in 2001. Since that reform, however, prosecutors have retained disproportionate power, and in non-jury trials a very high percentage of criminal cases result in convictions. Although the law entitles defendants to professional representation, defense lawyers are expensive and are lacking in some remote areas. President Vladimir Putin frequently has exempted government officials and wealthy businessmen from prosecution, even for very serious offenses. Under pressure from the European Union, Russia has not applied the death penalty since 1996, although that punishment retains legal standing. Beginning in 2004, jury trials have been held for the most serious offenses in all jurisdictions except the Republic of Chechnya. That year a new law defined for the first time the role and status of jurors. In recent years, clear procedural irregularities have been observed in well-publicized criminal cases such as the tax evasion trial of oil magnate Mikhail Khodorkovskiy (2004–5). In 2006 the Putin government proposed a US$1.8 billion, five-year program to reform Russia's judicial system from 2007 to 2011.

Electoral System: Suffrage is universal, and the minimum voting age is 18. Elections are organized and overseen by the 15-member Central Election Commission. The president, the State Duma, and the Federation Council each appoint five commission members to four-year terms. According to the constitution, the chairman of that commission, since 1999 Aleksandr Veshnyakov, is third in Russia's leadership line behind the president and the prime minister. The 89 subnational jurisdictions have equivalent commissions, which in turn oversee some 2,700 regional election commissions. The president and members of the Duma are elected by direct ballot to four-year terms. The last presidential election (normally held in March) was in 2004; the last parliamentary elections (normally in December) were held in 2003. The last regional and local elections were held in March 2006. The next parliamentary elections are scheduled for December 2007, the next presidential election for March 2008.

In 2006 the single-member constituencies that had elected half (225) of the Duma members were abolished, instead awarding all seats according to national party vote totals and eliminating the possibility of independents gaining seats. To achieve representation, a party must gain at least 7 percent of total votes. The presidential election includes a runoff between the top two vote-getters if no candidate gains a majority on the first ballot. Direct elections also choose legislatures at the subnational levels, although the president has the power to dissolve such legislatures and force the holding of new elections. Chief executives at those levels are appointed

21

by the president. National electoral reforms in 2005, all aiming to reduce opposition party strength, increased the minimum vote percentage required for a party to be represented in the Duma from 5 to 7 percent, prohibited parties from forming electoral coalitions, and stiffened party registration requirements.

Political Conditions and Parties: Aside from the Communist Party, a remnant of the Soviet era, Russia has had few political parties with national followings. In the immediate post-Soviet years, a wide variety of new parties espoused either some type of Western-style democratic and free-market reform or retaining a form of the strong central government inherited from Soviet times. Parliamentary elections of the 1990s generally fragmented and weakened the reform parties, although State Duma legislation in that period most often was the result of compromise. In that period, party configurations changed rapidly as groups merged and split. In 2001 the United Russia Party was formed, giving the Putin administration an effective voice in the Duma; that party's triumph in the 2003 parliamentary elections enhanced Putin's position. In those elections, the failure of any reform party to exceed the 5 percent minimum diminished the already weak political voice of the reform opposition. Ensuing legislation increased the minimum to 7 percent and required parties to have at least 50,000 members and organizations in at least half of Russia's regions, further enhancing the dominance of the United Russia Party. The major reform parties of the early 2000s, Yabloko and the Union of Rightist Forces, were hindered by the electoral reforms of 2005. A third reform party, the People's Democratic Union, appeared in 2006. In mid-2006, the reform parties discussed uniting into a single organization to ensure representation in the Duma. The Liberal Democratic Party of Russia and Rodina (Homeland) parties have nationalist agendas that include abolition of the federal system and expulsion of immigrants. In 2005 Rodina was the fastest growing party in Russia, but it was prohibited from participating in most regional elections in 2006.

Mass Media: After strict state control during most of the Soviet era, substantial media diversification began in the late 1980s, and during the Yeltsin presidency (1991–2000) most issues were discussed openly in the press and in the broadcast media. However, as wealthy entrepreneurs concentrated media resources, nonpartisan reporting became increasingly rare. Media control by pro-Yeltsin factions was cited as a major factor in Yeltsin's re-election as president in 1996. The role of the broadcast media has become more problematic during the Putin presidency. This is especially true because television, which was privatized and expanded rapidly in the 1990s, is the chief source of news for most Russians, and virtually all households have a television set.

Since 2000 the Putin administration has exerted strong pressure on independent television outlets in an effort to recentralize the media after the diversification of the 1990s. By 2004 all opposition television news programming had been forced off the air, and topics such as the Chechnya conflict have been covered from the government perspective only. The two largest national channels, ORT and Channel One, are state-owned and reach more than 95 percent of Russia's territory. Under new management, NTV, the last major independent television outlet, curbed its political commentary in 2004. The government owns the two most powerful radio stations, Radio Mayak and Radio Rossiya. In mid-2006, the government greatly reduced the availability of Voice of America and Radio Liberty broadcasts over Russian stations.

Following the crackdown on the broadcast media, newspapers have been the only source of media criticism of the government. As the broadcast media expanded, however, circulation of newspapers decreased because of production costs and competition from television, and in the early 2000s the number of independent print-media voices diminished steadily. Three publications that appeared after 1991, *Kommersant*, *Nazivisimaya Gazeta*, and *Novaya Gazeta*, maintained independent positions, although by 2006 the first two had muted their criticism of the government. In 2005 Gazprom-Media, the media branch of the state-owned Gazprom energy company, purchased the national daily *Izvestiya*, transforming it from a respected and balanced publication to a tabloid newspaper. The other major national newspapers are *Argumenty i Fakty*, *Izvestiya*, *Komsomol'skaya Pravda*, *Moskovskiy Komsomolets*, *Moskovskiye Novosti*, *Pravda*, and *Trud*. The *Moscow Times* and the *St. Petersburg Times* are major English-language newspapers. Outside Moscow and St. Petersburg, newspapers are controlled by local governments, most of which under the present political system are loyal to the Putin administration. In the early 2000s, free newspapers devoted mainly to advertising expanded their readership quickly in the large urban centers. The principal news agencies are ITAR–TASS, RIA Novosti (both government-owned), and Interfax. All major foreign news agencies have offices in Russia. Since 2001 several print journalists have been attacked or killed, allegedly because of their writings.

Foreign Policy: In the post-Soviet era, Russia's foreign relations have gone through several stages. In the early 1990s, Russia sought friendly relations with virtually all countries, especially the West and Japan. By the mid-1990s, a nationalist faction discouraged relations with the West in favor of renewed influence in the "Near Abroad" (the territory of the former Soviet Union) and closer ties with China. The two contradictory approaches have defined Russia's foreign policy since that time. In the mid-1990s, the expansion of the North Atlantic Treaty Organization (NATO) and the first of two conflicts with the Republic of Chechnya strained relations with the West. The September 11, 2001, terrorist attacks realigned Russia with the United States, but new strains came from the continuation of the second Chechnya conflict, Russia's support of Iran's nuclear program, and Russia's failure to support the U.S. invasion of Iraq in 2003. Meanwhile, Russia improved its position in the Near Abroad by strengthening relationships with Armenia, Azerbaijan, Kyrgyzstan, and Tajikistan and maintaining bases in Moldova and Georgia. In 2005 relations with Uzbekistan improved as that country reversed its earlier movement toward the West. Relations with Ukraine deteriorated after Ukraine elected a Western-oriented president in 2004 and Russia raised natural gas prices in 2005. Tension with Georgia increased in mid-2006 as Russia backed the demands of separatists in Georgia's South Ossetia region. Russia has used its role as natural gas supplier to gain leverage over both Georgia and Ukraine. Intensifying its commercial and diplomatic role in Asia, Russia has been a strong supporter of the six-nation Shanghai Cooperation Organization, which it sees as a key factor in blocking U.S influence in Central Asia, and it has improved relations with North and South Korea and China in a number of areas. However, in 2006 Russia's insistence on maintaining control of the Kuril Islands, a reversal of recent conciliation, chilled relations with Japan.

In the early 2000s, the Putin Administration continued to attempt a balance between restoring Russia's influence in the Near Abroad (particularly Central Asia, the Caucasus, and Ukraine) and preserving positive relations with the West, which has looked with disfavor on Russia's nationalistic ambitions. In that period, Russia's perceived support of regimes in Iran and Syria,

23

Western support for successful democratic movements in Georgia and Ukraine, Western criticism of Putin's policies toward Chechnya, and restriction of nongovernmental organizations and the media were issues that damaged the bilateral rapport achieved in 2001. In August 2006, the United States irked Russia by imposing sanctions on two Russian arms companies for their dealings with Iran. In 2006 Russia made progress in negotiations for membership in the World Trade Organization, but some issues caused the United States to delay approval of Russia's membership. The continued existence of the U.S. Jackson–Vanik Amendment, which originally linked U.S.-Soviet trade with the Soviet Union's emigration policy for Jews, also is a source of tension. In mid-2006, Russia enhanced its international prestige by hosting the annual Group of Eight summit meeting. Russia has used its veto power in the United Nations Security Council to influence international responses to crises in Iran, Sudan, and the Middle East.

Membership in International Organizations: Russia is a member of numerous international organizations, including the Arctic Council, Asia Pacific Economic Cooperation [sic], Association of Southeast Asian Nations (ASEAN, as a dialog partner and member of the ASEAN Regional Forum), Bank for International Settlements, Black Sea Economic Cooperation Pact, Central Asian Cooperation Organization (since 2004), Commonwealth of Independent States, Council of Baltic States, Council of Europe, Euro-Atlantic Partnership Council, European Bank for Reconstruction and Development, Group of Eight, International Atomic Energy Agency, International Bank for Reconstruction and Development, International Civil Aviation Organization, International Criminal Police Organization, International Federation of Red Cross and Red Crescent Societies, International Labour Organization, International Maritime Organization, International Monetary Fund, International Organization for Migration (as an observer), International Telecommunication Union, North Atlantic Treaty Organization, Partnership for Peace, Nuclear Suppliers Group, Organization for Security and Co-operation in Europe, Paris Club, Shanghai Cooperation Organization, United Nations Committee on Trade and Development, United Nations High Commissioner for Refugees, United Nations Industrial Development Organization, United Nations Institute for Training and Research, United Nations Security Council, Universal Postal Union, World Health Organization, and World Trade Organization (as an observer).

Major International Treaties: Russia is a signatory to numerous multilateral treaties, including the Basel Convention on the Control of Transboundary Movements of Hazardous Wastes and Their Disposal; Convention on Long-Range Transboundary Air Pollution; Convention on the International Trade in Endangered Species of Wild Flora and Fauna; Convention on the Prevention of Marine Pollution by Dumping Wastes and Other Matter (London Convention); Convention on the Prohibition of the Development, Production, and Stockpiling of Bacteriological (Biological) and Toxin Weapons and on Their Destruction; Convention on the Prohibition of the Development, Production, Stockpiling, and Use of Chemical Weapons and on Their Destruction; Geneva Convention (1949); International Convention for the Regulation of Whaling; International Covenant on Economic, Social and Cultural Rights; International Tropical Timber Agreement; Montreal Protocol on Substances that Deplete the Ozone Layer; Ramsar Convention; Treaty Banning Nuclear Weapons Tests in the Atmosphere, in Outer Space, and Under Water; Treaty on the Non-Proliferation of Nuclear Weapons; United Nations Convention on the Law of the Sea; and United Nations Framework Convention on Climate Change and its Kyoto protocol. Russia also has signed a number of bilateral arms control treaties with the United States on the limitation of strategic arms, antiballistic missile systems, and underground nuclear weapons tests and on the elimination of intermediate-range and shorter-range missiles.

NATIONAL SECURITY

Armed Forces Overview: The main branches of Russia's armed forces are the ground forces, navy, air forces, and strategic deterrent forces. In 2005 Russia had 1,027,000 active military personnel and about 20 million reservists. Of the active-duty personnel, about 250,000 were conscripts. The number of women has increased since contract service was introduced; estimates of their numbers varied from 115,000 to 160,000. Some 395,000 personnel were in the army, 142,000 in the navy (including 35,000 in naval aviation), 160,000 in the air forces, and 80,000 in the strategic deterrent forces, whose total manpower of 129,000 also included 38,000 air force and 11,000 navy personnel. About 40,000 of the strategic deterrent forces were classified as strategic missile force troops. Another 250,000 active personnel were designated for command and support duties. Russia has an ongoing military reform program that is to include streamlining and professionalization of all units—goals widely recognized as necessary to meet Russia's post-Soviet military needs at a time when the military manpower pool is diminishing. However, troop dissatisfaction and low funding have hampered expansion of this program beyond individual units. Reforms also may rearrange the military districts and the status of the main branches. The Chechnya conflict, which decreased in intensity in 2006, damaged morale throughout the military and exposed planners' inability to adapt existing doctrine to nonconventional combat. Domestic ground forces are divided into six military districts: Moscow, Leningrad, Volga, North Caucasus, Siberian, and Far Eastern. The navy is divided into four fleets (Northern, Black Sea, Pacific, and Baltic) and the Caspian Sea Flotilla. A new military doctrine was scheduled to replace the existing (2002) doctrine in 2007, enumerating more precisely Russia's national security position and the threats to it.

Foreign Military Relations: In the early 2000s, China and India have been the top customers for Russia's military exports, which in 2005 reached a new high of US$6.1 billion. In 2005 Russia and China held their first-ever joint military exercises on the coast of China's Shandong Province, and in 2006 plans called for continued sales of advanced arms to China. A treaty with the Association of Southeast Asian Nations includes a security partnership section. India plans extended military cooperation with Russian forces after conducting large-scale bilateral naval exercises in 2003. In the early 2000s, Russia intensified its military links in Central Asia. A comprehensive defense treaty with Uzbekistan in 2004 was followed by a 2005 mutual defense treaty. Bilateral defense treaties with Tajikistan ensured the long-term presence of the Russian troops that have been in Tajikistan throughout the post-Soviet era. In 2006 Russia tripled the number of aircraft stationed at its air base at Kant in Kyrgyzstan.

In 2005 and 2006, Russian forces participated in various joint exercises with forces of Armenia, Canada, India, Kyrgyzstan, Sweden, Turkey, and the United States. In early 2006, joint naval and antiterrorism exercises were held in the Ionian Sea to evaluate the interoperability of North Atlantic Treaty Organization (NATO) and Russian systems. The NATO–Russia Council provides Russia input into NATO policies, with the goal of alleviating stress over NATO expansion eastward. Russia is a signatory of the Global Partnership Against the Spread of Weapons and Materials of Mass Destruction. Russia receives aid from the United States, the United Kingdom, and the European Union for destruction of its chemical weapons in accord with the Chemical Weapons Convention. The Multilateral Nuclear Environmental Programme in the Russian Federation provides for European assistance projects in nuclear waste disposal.

External Threat: No conventional external threat exists. However, the stepwise expansion of the North Atlantic Treaty Organization (NATO) into Eastern Europe and the three Baltic states of the former Soviet Union has caused irritation in Russia, some of which has been alleviated by participation in the NATO–Russia Council and by a NATO promise not to deploy nuclear weapons in the new member countries.

Defense Budget: Russia's military outlays, particularly allocations among defense subcategories, are difficult to assess. Reportedly, the 2005 budget increased direct military spending by 28 percent over the 2004 total. Overall, between 2002 and 2005 estimated defense budgets increased from US$8.4 billion to US$17.7 billion. However, experts see drastic increases in the early 2000s as compensation for the substantial underfunding of the military in the late 1990s. Russia's high inflation also plays a role in the nominal increases. The military budget for 2006, calling for US$22.3 billion, was 25 percent larger than its predecessor, with a stronger emphasis on research and development and acquisition of arms and equipment. However, reorganization of national budget classifications in 2005 added some new types of expenditures to the traditional national defense categories. Among the latter, another US$4.5 billion was budgeted in 2006 for support functions such as military housing, health, and education. The draft budget for 2007 called for an increase of 23 percent in military spending, to US$30.4 billion. Increases targeted arms purchases, research and development, and a 10 percent pay raise for military personnel.

Major Military Units: The army has 5 tank divisions, 16 motorized rifle divisions, 4 airborne divisions, 5 machine gun and artillery divisions, 3 artillery divisions and 4 independent artillery brigades, 9 special forces brigades, 12 surface-to-surface missile brigades, 11 surface-to-air missile brigades, 5 antitank brigades, and 1 engineer brigade. The navy is divided into four fleets: the Baltic, Black Sea, Northern, and Pacific, each with its own fleet air force, plus the Caspian Sea Flotilla. The naval infantry (marines), 9,500 strong, includes three independent brigades and three special forces brigades. The air force is divided into two commands, the Long Range Aviation Command (57th Air Army) and the Military Transport Aviation Command (61st Air Army). The former command includes eight bomber regiments, the latter nine regiments. In addition, tactical aviation forces consist of five tactical and air defense armies totaling 49 air regiments. The strategic missile force is divided into three rocket armies.

Major Military Equipment: In the early 2000s, large numbers of major equipment items had outlived their service life, and replacement occurred at a much slower rate. In 2005 the army had 22,800 main battle tanks; 150 light tanks; 2,000 armored reconnaissance vehicles; 15,090 armored infantry fighting vehicles; 9,900 armored personnel carriers; 30,045 artillery pieces, including 6,010 self-propelled pieces, 6,100 mortars, and 4,350 multiple rocket launchers; 200 nuclear-capable surface-to-surface missiles; and 2,465 surface-to-air missiles. The navy had 46 tactical and 15 nuclear submarines, 1 aircraft carrier, 6 cruisers, 15 destroyers, 19 frigates, 26 corvettes, 41 mine warfare vessels, 22 major amphibious vessels, and 72 patrol and coastal combat vessels. The navy also had 266 combat aircraft. The air forces had 1,013 fighter aircraft, 677 bombers and ground-attack fighters, 119 reconnaissance aircraft, 293 military transport aircraft, and 1,520 helicopters. The strategic missile force had 570 launchers with 2,035 nuclear warheads. In 2006 the missile force added a first unit of advanced mobile Topol–M missiles. According to plans, that missile was to be the basis of significant new reliance on the missile force for conventional and antiterrorist defense in the period 2007–11. The nuclear submarines were equipped with a total of 252 missiles. In 2006 two new nuclear submarines carried Bulava missiles, Russia's first new intercontinental ballistic missile model in the post-Soviet era.

Military Service: Males between ages 18 and 27 are eligible to be conscripted for terms of 18 to 24 months. The reserve obligation extends to age 50. Legislation in 2006 called for the term of active duty to be reduced to one year in 2008. In recent years, the quantity and quality of recruits have dropped dramatically because of the Chechnya conflict, low pay, and adverse service conditions. In the air force draft of spring 2006, only 20 percent of conscripts were found fit for combat units. The tradition of hazing new recruits drew increased public criticism in the early 2000s, but the practice continued to discourage enlistment. In mid-2006 the Ministry of Defense announced that the first phase of the plan to create an all-volunteer armed force would conclude in 2008, with special emphasis on professionalizing the rank of sergeant (to reduce hazing) and personnel in airborne units and units designated for conflict. However, in 2006 large numbers of early contract cancellations reduced the prospects of meeting program goals.

Paramilitary Forces: In 2005 a total of 415,000 individuals were on active duty with paramilitary forces. This total included 160,000 in the Federal Border Guard Service, 170,000 in the five paramilitary divisions of the Ministry of Internal Affairs, and about 4,000 in the Federal Security Service. The Federal Protection Service, including the Presidential Guard Regiment, includes 10,000 to 30,000 troops. In 2006 the Federal Security Service added 300 counterterrorist personnel.

Military Forces Abroad: In 2006 Russian forces were stationed in several countries of the former Soviet Union: Armenia, Belarus, Georgia, Kyrgyzstan, Moldova, Tajikistan, and Ukraine. The presence of Russian forces, ostensibly as peacekeepers, in the separatist republics of Abkhazia and South Ossetia was an ongoing irritant in relations with Georgia. Russia has provided troops or observers for several United Nations (UN) peacekeeping groups: the Interim Administration Mission in Kosovo; the Mission for the United Nations Referendum in Western Sahara; the Mission in Ethiopia and Eritrea; the Mission in Sierra Leone; the Observer Mission in Georgia; and UN operations in Burundi, Congo, and Côte d'Ivoire.

Police: Russia's civilian police force, the militia, falls under the Ministry of Internal Affairs. Divided into public security units and criminal police, the militia is administered at federal, regional, and local levels. Security units, which are financed by local and regional funds, are responsible for routine maintenance of public order. The criminal police are divided into specialized units by type of crime. Among the latter units are the Main Directorate for Organized Crime and the Federal Tax Police Service. The latter agency now is independent. Since its establishment, the militia has been plagued by low pay, low prestige, and a high corruption level. The autonomous Federal Security Service, whose main responsibility is counterintelligence and counterterrorism, also has broad law enforcement powers. In early 2006, President Putin called for a wholesale review of police practices at the city, district, and transport levels.

Internal Threat: Increasingly sophisticated national and transnational criminal organizations are extremely active throughout Russia, especially in the Far East, Yekaterinburg, Moscow, and St. Petersburg. Criminal organizations control the trafficking of a wide variety of commodities. In urban centers, protection rackets prey on legitimate businesses. Russia is a vital link in narcotics smuggling from Afghanistan through Central Asia to Western Europe. Important factors in crime are government and police corruption, a growing domestic narcotics market, a weak judiciary, ineffective border controls, and the open, chaotic nature of post-Soviet commercial activity. Throughout the early 2000s, extremist nationalist groups such as the skinheads proliferated all over Russia, and the number of attacks on minority individuals increased sharply in 2005 and 2006. In 2006 skinhead membership was estimated at 70,000. In recent years, Russia's financial institutions have suffered a drastic increase in computer crimes. The 2005 federal budget substantially increased funds for security and law enforcement activities.

Insurgency and Terrorism: In 1999 a series of bomb attacks in population centers was attributed to Chechen separatists, leading to the resumption of conflict between Russian forces and Chechen guerrillas. In 2001 Russia strongly supported U.S. actions in response to the September 11 attacks, a position that brought the countries closer. In 2002 Chechen terrorists took about 600 Russians hostage in a Moscow theater, sharpening Russia's anti-Chechen and antiterrorism policy. Between 2002 and 2004, terrorist attacks in Russia killed an estimated 500 people. In May 2004, Chechen rebels assassinated Akhmad Kadyrov, the pro-Russian president of the Republic of Chechnya, and in September 2004 Chechen terrorists led by Shamil Basayev killed about 320 hostages at a Russian school in Beslan, near the border of Chechnya. In July 2006, Russian troops killed Basayev. Basayev's alleged links with al Qaeda and other foreign terrorist groups were uncertain. Basayev's death and the rise of Kadyrov's charismatic son as leader of Chechnya were expected to diminish the longstanding Chechen insurgency. The main remaining insurgent group, led by Dokka Umarov, staged terrorist attacks throughout the North Caucasus region in 2006. Throughout the early 2000s, the dubious security of Russia's substantial stock of nuclear materials caused international concern that a terrorist organization might obtain such materials in Russia. The 2005 budget substantially increased funds for Russia's antiterrorism programs, and in 2006 the Federal Security Service established counterterrorism committees at the national and regional levels.

Human Rights: The constitution of 1993 guarantees broad freedoms of speech, assembly, fair trial, and the press, as well as protection against deprivation of liberty and inhumane punishment. However, in practice many of those guarantees have been withheld. Human rights observers have reported the use of torture in prisons and against prisoners in the Chechen conflict. Police violence and extortion have been concentrated against Caucasian, Central Asian, and Roma individuals. Military servicemen continue to suffer violent "hazing" rituals. Prison conditions in general are harsh, and rates of death and contagious diseases such as tuberculosis and human immunodeficiency virus (HIV) among prisoners are very high. In 2004 some measures were taken to reduce prison overcrowding.

Arbitrary arrest and detention are frequent, and pretrial detention often is lengthy. However, authorities have increasingly complied with the detention limitations of the 2003 Criminal Procedure Code. The chief national law enforcement agency, the Federal Security Service, receives limited oversight by the federal procuracy and the courts. Ongoing, unrestricted use of force by troops against civilians in the Chechen conflict has been documented, despite restrictions on press coverage. Some religious groups have faced regional government restrictions under a 1997 law that regulates religious practice. Instances of prejudice and violence against Jews, Muslims, and other minorities increased in 2004. Nontraditional religions such as Jehovah's Witnesses and splinter Muslim groups have been deprived of official status, sometimes on security grounds. Recent national elections have been conducted fairly, but government control of the media has been criticized during campaigns, and interference with journalists has been common. The treatment of displaced persons in the Chechen conflict has come into question. Nongovernmental organizations (NGOs) have felt pressure and been subjected to occasional violence if they take controversial positions. In 2006 a controversial new agency, the Federal Registration Service, established a complex registration procedure for the estimated 400,000 foreign and domestic NGOs in Russia. As of October 2006, large numbers of significant NGOs had failed to fulfill agency requirements.

Crimes against women, including domestic violence and trafficking (both domestic and to other countries), are frequent. Because there is no law against sexual harassment, women have no recourse in such situations. Child abuse and trafficking in children also are significant problems.

www.ingramcontent.com/pod-product-compliance
Lightning Source LLC
Chambersburg PA
CBHW080800290526
45790CB00008B/3526